WHAT ELSE CAN YOU DO?

By JEAN MARZOLLO

Pictures by JERRY PINKNEY

The Bodley Head · London

British Library Cataloguing in Publication Data

Marzollo, Jean
What else can you do?
I. Title II. Pinkney, Jerry
813'.54 [J]
ISBN 0-370-31457-3

Printed in Hong Kong by South China Printing Company (1988) Limited for
The Bodley Head Children's Books
20 Vauxhall Bridge Road,
London SW1V 2SA

First published in Great Britain in 1990
by The Bodley Head Children's Books
Originally published in the United States in 1990
under the title *Pretend You're a Cat* by
Dial Books for Young Readers, a division of Penguin Books USA Inc.
Published by arrangement with Dial Books for Young Readers.

*The full-colour artwork was prepared using
pencil, coloured pencils, and watercolour.
It was then colour-separated and reproduced as
red, blue, yellow, and black halftones.*

Can you climb?
Can you leap?
Can you stretch?
Can you sleep?

Can you hiss?
Can you pat?
Can you purr
Like a cat?

What else can you do like a cat?

Can you bark?
Can you beg?
Can you scratch
With your leg?

Can you fetch?
Can you roll?
Can you dig
In a hole?

What else can you do like a dog?

Can you jump?
Can you leap?
Can you swim
As you sleep?

Can you nibble
And look
At a worm
On a hook?

What else can you do like a fish?

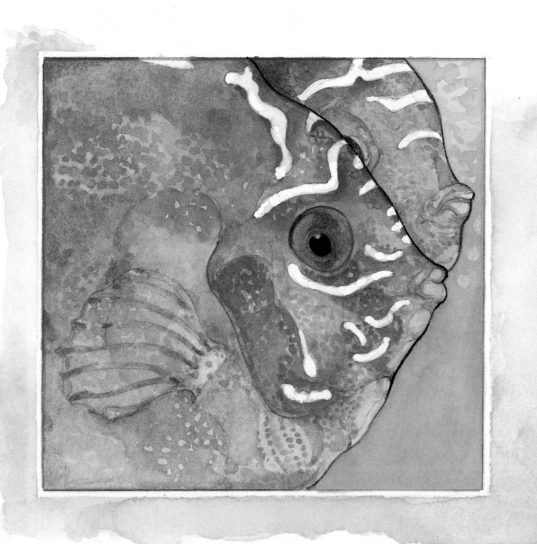

Can you fly?
Can you buzz?
Are you covered
With fuzz?

Can you land
On my knee?
Can you sting
Like a bee?

What else can you do like a bee?

Can you peck?
Can you pick
At a shell
Like a chick?

Can you scratch?
Can you cheep?
Can you hop?
Can you peep?

What else can you do like a chick?

Can you perch?
Can you fly?
Can you soar
In the sky?

Can you chirp?
Can you sing?
Can you flap
With your wings?

What else can you do like a bird?

Can you chatter
And flee?
Disappear
In a tree?

Can you run?
Can you twirl?
Can you leap
Like a squirrel?

What else can you do like a squirrel?

Are you pink
As a bud?
Can you lie
In the mud?

Can you squeal?
Can you dig?
Can you snort
Like a pig?

What else can you do like a pig?

Can you chew?
Can you munch?
Can you moo
During lunch?

Can you drink
from a pail?
Touch your ear
With your tail?

What else can you do like a cow?

Can you snort?
Can you neigh?
Can you eat
Grain and hay?

Can you open
The gate?
Can you run
With your mate?

What else can you do like a horse?

Can you balance
A ball
On your nose
And not fall?

Can you dive
For your meal?
Can you bark
Like a seal?

What else can you do like a seal?

Can you wiggle
And glide?
Can you slither
And slide?

Can you head
For the lake?
Can you swim
Like a snake?

What else can you do like a snake?

Are you big?
Are you brave?
Can you sleep
In a cave?

Can you sniff
At the air?
Can you roar
Like a bear?

What else can you do like a bear?